GETTING INTO THE ZONE

A COURSE and WORKBOOK
For the Mental Game

Written by: Elliot and Kathy Hagburg

This book is dedicated to all of the unaware and unenlightened, coaches, teachers, and bosses. Without all of the lemons they provide, we could never have created this wonderful batch of lemonade. Without you, this book and workshop could never have been born. For this we thank you.

Foreword

A game changer is a defining moment, event or idea that creates an instantaneous momentum shift of energy. It can be a positive, "poetry in motion" energy shift, or a negative, "slip on a banana peel" energy shift. The catalyst for either of these energy exchanges is our thoughts or the collective thoughts of a group or team. It triggers a chain of events or outcomes, which are based on the outlooks and beliefs of the observers/participants. This energy is flowing and circulating through us at all times. We also have complete access to it at all times. By training our minds, we can learn to achieve top performance and create the ultimate game changer. Once we realize we are more than just flesh and bones, we can begin to take control of our lives , both on and off the playing field. WARNING, Do not attempt to read this book unless you are prepared to be the Star you always dreamed of being.

"All the world is a stage
And all men and women merely actors:
They have their exits and entrances;
And one man in his time plays many
parts, his acts being seven stages."

William Shakespeare

Welcome to our "Mental Workshop"
We are happy you decided to join us.
We believe you are holding in your hands,
the missing piece of your athletic training
puzzle.   Although, this course is designed
for young athletes, the principles can be
applied to all areas of life.   The good news
is: you can begin exactly where you are,
regardless of your current level of skill. By
reading the course and completing the
workbook exercises, we fully expect you to
begin enjoying the results you desire.
Remember to enjoy the journey.

Let's get started!

NOTES

What Percentage of your athletic training is devoted to:

Hitting _____ %

Strength/
Conditioning _____ %

Baseball
Practice _____ %

Games _____ %

TOTAL 100 %

How much of the game do you believe is
Mental _____%

Most experts will tell you it's 80%

If the game is 80% mental . . . .

What percentage of your time is devoted to
building a winning attitude? _____ %

This workshop will train you to develop the
mental game - to match your physical skills.

NOTES

Your life is meant to be fun, exciting and colorful. It should be bursting with all of the thrilling twists and turns of a Hollywood blockbuster. What is your favorite movie or blockbuster? _____

Think about what you love most about it. Is it the type of story that has you on the edge of your seat? Maybe it's a Comedy, so funny you laugh till you cry. Perhaps it's a Love Story or a Thriller. Most likely, it's a combination of thrills, chills, romance, comedy, and drama. Your "life story" should be nothing less. It should be a "sold out", "standing room only" spectacular. More importantly, you should be the star!

NOTES

To be the STAR of your own Blockbuster..

The process is as follows:

1. Choosing your Role
        (What do you really want?)

2. Writing the Script
        (The Conscious and Sub-conscious
            Mind)

3. Painting the Set
        (Visualization)

4. Rehearsing you lines
        (Affirmations)

5. Yell Cut!
        (Learning to press pause)

6. Enjoy the Movie
        (Visual Motor Rehearsal)

7. Standing Ovations
        (Gratitude)

NOTES

"If you don't know where you are going you might end up someplace else."

Yogi Berra

Welcome to your own Blockbuster . . .

1.   **Choosing your Role** or deciding what you really want.

Do you want to be the Hero? The Villain? The Victim? The Clown?

Throughout most of our early lives, our roles are assigned or handed to us by our Parents, Teachers and experiences.

Are you aware you can change roles at any time?   It's your turn to choose. Answer the following question:

Since we can have, do, or be anything: What do you really want to have, do, change, or experience? For example; What type of athlete do you want to be? What type of person do you desire to be and how would you like others to describe you?

"If you build it, he will come."

Shoeless Joe Jackson
Field of Dreams

2. WRITING THE SCRIPT

Although you have one mind, there are two
parts to it:
Conscious Mind - The Chooser.
> Objective. The gatekeeper to the
> subconscious mind.

The Subconscious- The order taker.
> Subjective. It automatically creates
> scenarios based on what the
> gatekeeper tells it.

Your Conscious mind decides.
The Subconscious mind carries out orders.
Thoughts and ideas become things. Simply
put, the subconscious mind is the auto-pilot
acting out people, places, things and events
based on the beliefs held by the Conscious
mind.

This is the part I so want you to get. If your
gatekeeper (conscious mind) is untrained
and inexperienced, unwanted guests
(beliefs) will slip through the gate.

NOTES

These unwanted guests are unproductive beliefs.

Here is an example to illustrate this point. A young player loves baseball and dreams of playing in the "big leagues" some day. He shares this dream freely with his friends, family, and teachers. For reasons only they could know, somebody tells him, "Oh, you have to be over 6 feet tall to make it in the Majors. You will never be tall enough."

Now, there is absolutely no truth to that statement! There are plenty of average size players in Major League baseball. However, if this player's gatekeeper (conscious mind) entertains the idea "I'll never be tall enough" and accepts it as true, this seed or unproductive belief is now planted in his subconscious mind. Any repetition of this thought will cause it to take root and begin to grow.

Our player still loves baseball. He still loves to play and practice. He takes hitting lessons, catching lessons and fielding lessons. He is physically prepared and ready to excel. However, he has been

NOTES

thinking about the idea "I'll never be tall enough" ever since he first heard it. He wonders if he's wasting his time with all these lessons, since he has no reason to believe he will ever be close to 6 feet tall.

He decides to try out for an All Star team. During the tryout his subconscious mind (the order taker) proceeds to sabotage his performance. It says, "You can't do this, you're too short." After a rather poor tryout his conscious mind adds another unwanted guest, " maybe, I'm not good enough!"

Of course, the subconscious mind now responds, "OK, you're too short AND you're not good enough. Anything else?" It is not discerning. The subconscious just gobbles up whatever we feed it and translates it into events and circumstances that match what our conscious mind tells it. Therefore, if we are sporting unproductive beliefs, we must uproot them via reprogramming if we want to experience a different result.

A good place to start is by identifying any unproductive beliefs you may already have.

NOTES

For example: I'm not good enough.
                I'm a lousy test taker.
                I never feel good

Try to honestly list at least 3 unproductive beliefs that you have in your life. They don't have to be sports related. Take your time and be as honest as you can with yourself.

_____
_____
_____
_____
_____
_____
_____
_____

Looking back at the example responses we used before, what would the subconscious script be for a person whose beliefs are; I'm not good enough? I'm a lousy test taker? I never feel good? This person's subconscious mind will be saying, "You're a lousy test taker. You aren't good enough anyway. You don't deserve to feel good."

NOTES

Our subconscious minds will act out the story/script we unknowingly provide with our thoughts. A person can study 24/7 and not succeed until he extracts "I'm a lousy test taker" and plants "I'm a terrific test taker" in its place. It is important that any new thoughts or ideas, especially those that are presented to us by other people, be challenged and found to be to our benefit, before they are allowed through the gate.

The Subconscious does not know the difference between "real" or "make-believe". A picture of an apple or an actual apple = apple.

Computer programmers have a saying:
Garbage in = Garbage out
Therefore, becoming aware of your habit of thought is key. Your *self-talk* or things you say to yourself on a regular basis is a good indicator of your habit of thought.

Is your self-talk positive or negative? Are you nicer to others than you are to yourself?

NOTES

If you say things to yourself like: "I can't hit a curveball" or "nothing works out for me", chances are you are working from a negative script and it's time for a re-write. We all fall into this mode of thinking from time to time, but the key is to become aware of our thoughts so we can make quick adjustments along the way.

Begin re-writing your Script/story

Write about everything you would like to experience in the present tense (the zone) in every area of your life. Be descriptive enough to get all your senses involved.

Here is MY script/story:

I am so thrilled and thankful now that.....
I am a tall, handsome, physically fit young man. I am well educated. I have a passion for baseball. I am fascinated with the "mental game". I teach young players, coaches, and parents to master it. I am traveling around the world teaching my workshops-helping young people improve their lives and performance. I am so thrilled to be able to work from anywhere and decide how often I work. I am extremely creative-producing

NOTES

products and tools to inspire and enhance the learning process. I am dating a smart, beautiful woman. She is educated, a team player. She has a successful business of her own. She has blond hair, hazel eyes, and a peaches and cream complexion. She loves baseball as much as I do. I have a terrific waterfront home. I love the sound of the waves and the smell of the ocean. (you get the idea)

Now you are ready to begin your new script/story:
I am so thrilled and thankful now that . . .

_____

_____

_____

_____

_____

_____

_____

_____

_____

_____

_____

_____

_____

_____

_____

"The man who has no imagination has no wings."

Muhammed Ali

3.   PAINTING THE SET (Visualization)

This is where you get to be that five or six year old kid again. Remember when you pretended? Haven't you pictured yourself with bases loaded hitting that walk-off homerun? Or, in a Major League stadium getting the chance to be the hero for thousands of home team fans?

Bring your story to life by thinking in mental pictures. Be sure to include colors, sounds, smells, emotions etc.   Remember, your subconscious mind will think it's real. Picture every part of your story as if it has already happened. TIP: Don't cheat yourself here…THINK BIG! Picture yourself doing great things you might never have thought possible before!

NOTES

Vision Boards

Create your story with pictures. Use your own artwork, photos, or cut and paste magazine pictures. Arrange your collage on corkboard or poster board. Some examples would be: a picture of your dream car, an acceptance letter to the College of your choice, your dream prom date, you holding the MVP trophy, your desired SAT score, etc. Be creative! Try creating some of your own pictures with paint or markers. Drawing, painting or coloring draws you into the zone, instantly. Display your vision board in full view. Make sure it's the first thing you see in the morning and the last thing you see at night. Take a picture of it with your phone and make it your wallpaper. Carry it with you, never losing sight of your vision. Every time you look at it, generate the joyful feelings and emotions that correspond to having it already. Act as if it's already happened. Remember to think BIG. Nothing is off limits. Don't judge or worry about how it's going to happen or any of the details. Your job is only to get excited about your creation. The Universe will take care of the details.

NOTES

"It's a funny thing, the more I practice the luckier I get".

Arnold Palmer

4. REHEARSING YOUR LINES

Dr. Dennis Waitly trained NASA astronauts for high performance. He later adapted the same program for Olympic athletes.

He had Olympic athletes run their race/event in their minds while hooked up to biofeedback machines. What he discovered is: the same muscles fired in their bodies during the mental rehearsal as did in the actual race. The mind could not differentiate between the real or simulated event.

Try this: Picture a plump, yellow, juicy lemon. Picture yourself cutting it in half. Take one half and take a big bite out of it.

Is your mouth watering?
Did you lips pucker up?

This process is called VMH or Visual Motor Rehearsal.

NOTES

It is important to relax and get into the present (the zone) before rehearsing your script.

Relaxation: Inhale deeply (four counts) Exhale (four counts) repeat five times. Starting at your feet, consciously tell your feet to relax, slowly move to calves, knees, thighs, hips, abs, chest, arms, shoulders, neck and head. When you feel relaxed, start rehearsing your lines/script. This is done every night before falling asleep and every morning before you get out of bed. Soon you will have learned your lines and not need your actual script in front of you.

Most Psychologists agree: It takes 28 days to change a habit. Conducting this exercise morning and evening, plus any bonus rehearsals you might add, will move your story from the conscious to the subconscious or auto-pilot. In a short time you will be totally in character. It is important your self-talk matches the role you've chosen.

NOTES

Example: If you have chosen to be the Hero in your story (I hope you have), it is important to choose your words carefully. Remember, thoughts become things. Never complete a negative thought. By sticking to your script, you can avoid the old habit of negative self-talk.

Muhammed Ali, the greatest boxer of all time, only spoke about what he wanted in the present tense. Long before he became the Heavyweight champion of the world, he would enter every arena chanting: "The Champ is here"! When interviewed, he always replied: "I am the greatest"! He made up rhymes (affirmations) and recited them constantly-regarding specific opponents. He pictured each fight in his mind before the actual event. If he made a mistake-he would re-play the scene is his mind with the outcome he desired.

Notice Ali said "I am" not "I will be"! Since we can only perform in the PRESENT, why not think in the present as well?

NOTES

Granted, you may not need to take it as far as Ali, and shout it out in public, but this kind of talk is certainly appropriate when we are speaking to ourselves! Go ahead and say it out loud to yourself. Get used to it so you can start really believing it!

I had the pleasure of meeting, Bucky Dent, former Yankee shortstop during my years at Hofstra University. His affirmation was: "If the ball comes to me, you're out!" He went on to say, "humans do not function efficiently when they are tense. Relax, have fun, and let the game come to you." To quote Jack Elliot, in the film, Mr. Baseball, "Baseball is a game, and games are supposed to be fun."

What are affirmations? They are the seeds of success you have just planted. Picture your seeds in full bloom. Do not allow the weeds of doubt or fear to choke or infiltrate your garden. If you plant a watermelon seed you expect to get a watermelon. You wouldn't start worrying about it becoming a pumpkin or a squash. You would patiently feed and nurture it daily while it takes root. During this process, you would picture yourself slicing into your juicy watermelon and taking that first sweet bite of the season.

NOTES

Create some affirmations for yourself in the present tense. Remember, something your character would say in a positive format:

Examples: I am a 400 Hitter.
           I am getting better every day.
           I am a Division I caliber player.

_____
_____
_____
_____
_____
_____
_____
_____
_____
_____
_____
_____
_____
_____
_____
_____

Preparing your garden. . .

If you've gotten this far, we'll assume you already have a physical training schedule for: strength, agility, speed, and flexibility. The mind, also needs to be exercised regularly in order to train it. Begin by perceiving your mind as a tool. Like a pencil, a saw, or a chef's knife; each needs to be sharpened. More importantly, they are put down when not in use. These exercises, once mastered, will keep your "tool" sharpened and allow you to put it down when it's not being used. You will need to create your "mind gym" in a quiet spot or room where you won't be disturbed. You will need a comfortable straight backed chair, a timer or phone alarm.

Mind Exercise #1

Set a timer for 5 minutes
Sit in your chair with feet flat on the floor. Rest your hands, palms up on your thighs. Sit still for 5 minutes. Thoughts will come and go. Let them come. Be a still, silent observer. This exercise will give you the first glimpse of how noisy your mind is. It will also train you to be still. Do this exercise daily until you have mastered it.

NOTES

Mind Exercise # 2

Once you have mastered exercise #1,
go to your "mind gym." Set the timer for 5
minutes. Sit comfortably in your chair.
Begin breathing in for 4 counts, exhale 4
counts. Repeat the breathing throughout the
exercise. Put all of your focus on your
breathing. If a thought pops up, gently bring
your attention back to your breathing.
Practice this daily until you have mastered it.
Once you feel you have achieved a place of
"non - thinking", begin adding 1 minute per
day until you are able to do the exercise for
10 minutes. Consistency is critical. You
didn't develop strong biceps or a "six pack"
overnight. A regular training schedule is
required.

Once you have exercised your mind to a
place of "non - thinking", you are In The
Zone. It is the space in the present
moment, where all power, inspiration, and
creation takes place.

This is the place, Babe Ruth, went to before
he pointed his bat at the centerfield fence.
It is where Beethoven wrote his symphonies,
and Michelangelo sculpted "David".

NOTES

"Pay no attention to that man behind the curtain."

The Wizard
The Wizard of Oz

5.   YELL CUT! (learning to press pause)

Most of us have been trained negatively. Teachers mark our test papers with ugly red Xs. Imagine if instead, they put smiley faces on the correct answers-ignoring the mistakes. It would change our whole education experience. Coaches, without an understanding of the "mental game", tend to harp on errors with no honorable mention of the highlights. Parents, unknowingly make comments - planting unproductive seeds (beliefs): "you're lazy", "put your coat on-you'll catch a cold" "make sure you have something to fall back on if this doesn't work out." None of these statements are true - you've just adopted them through repetition. Beliefs are nothing more than thoughts you think over and over.   The good news is: You can plant new positive seeds (beliefs) the same way.

Yelling cut or pressing the pause button will enable you to catch yourself when old worn out thoughts pop up. Retraining yourself to

NOTES

respond instead of react is a skill.
Fortunately, you have a built-in GPS . . .

Your emotions!

Once you have rehearsed your script, your
emotions will tell you instantly if you are in or
out of character.

Example: If you feel good, calm, joyful, and
expecting good things-you are totally in
character.   If you feel fear, doubt, or anger-
you've deviated from your script.

When feeling negative emotions . . .

Yell cut!   Press pause and choose to
respond the way your character would.
Remember . . . In every great blockbuster,
the hero's response to all situations is what
sets him apart.

The Hero always brings his/her focus back
to what he wants.   The Victim focuses on
the worst case scenario.   The Hero talks
only of the outcome he/she expects.   The
Victim holds pity parties-constantly talking
about "how bad things are".   The Hero lives

NOTES

in the present.   The Victim lives in the past
or future, never in the moment.

If your old character tries to sneak back in,
go back and re-read your script.   Do the
relaxation exercises and get back on track.

Every actor in the early stages of performing
has experienced, hecklers, i.e. Coaches,
fans, parents etc.   As his confidence in his
performance grows, he is soon able to
ignore them. Soon, they disappear.   The
performance, when polished, is now an
inside job.   The heckling transforms into
standing ovations.

Remember-what seems to be "outside
negativity" is their story - not yours.
The best reaction is *No* reaction.

NOTES

Blackbird singing in the dead of night
Take these sunken eyes and learn to see
All your life, you were only waiting for this *moment*
to be free.

Paul McCartney

6. ENJOYING THE MOVIE
   (The Law of attraction)

The Law of attraction is a Universal Law that states: Like attracts like. Birds of feather, stick together. Positive people attract positive people. It works every time for every person.

Once you are so rehearsed, you are giving "Oscar performances", the Law of Attraction will draw to you opportunities, events, and people matching what you are asking for.

The better it gets, the better it gets.

Unfortunately, it works both ways. Have you ever played in this game? Everything's going great! It's late in the game. The pitcher is throwing a gem and the score is close, with your team ahead by a run. The shortstop bobbles a routine ground ball, scrambles, and then overthrows first. Now

NOTES

the tying run is on second. The shortstop is having a private tantrum, the first baseman is screaming at the shortstop, and the coach is screaming at everybody on the field from the dugout! Chaos has now replaced the confidence the team felt just moments ago. Negative energy now attracts more negative energy and the game spirals out of control.

If only the players and coach had known how to "press pause"! If only they had known to remain calm, take a deep breath, and refocus on their desired outcome. Positive thoughts would have just as naturally attracted positive energy and a positive outcome.

This part is critical. Your old character may have gotten angry, kicked the dirt and made a critical comment to himself in a situation like this. However, The Hero learns to stop, take a deep breath, and mentally rehearse the play again with the outcome he desires. He positively intends to get the next one.

NOTES

"Appreciation is a wonderful thing. It makes what is excellent in others belong to us as well."

Voltaire

7. APPLAUSE (GRATITUDE)

One of the best ways to get more of what you want is to show appreciation for yourself and others. Gratitude always attracts more of what you want to you. When Mom prepares your favorite dinner, a standing ovation will guarantee more of them!

Find something to be grateful for each and every day. Show appreciation as often as possible. Pay compliments-ignore criticism. You are attracting to you - whatever you put "out there".
In other words, if you want:

Inspiration	- Inspire someone
Love	- Say I love you often, especially when looking in the mirror
Money	- Be generous
Success	- Help other people get what they want

NOTES

As you become the master of your blockbuster, you'll learn to applaud (show gratitude) when you experience what you want. If something is not part of your story, you will learn to ignore it. One by one your experiences will begin to shift and match "your story". As you grow and change, you can amend and add new experiences to your movie.

Playing with sweaty palms (showstoppers)

The biggest dream breaker is fear.
Fear is nothing more than the anticipation of an unpleasant future event, or old thoughts of past events. Fear can not exist in _the zone_ or the _present moment._ If you are focused in the _now,_ fear can not creep in. If you're thinking of your last "at bat", even if it was fantastic, you are remembering a past event. Once you have visualized your next play, pitch, or hit , let it go and go to your place of non-thinking. Allow your auto-pilot (subconscious mind) to take over.

Get out of your own way! Don't begin unless you can _see_ it first. That's what "time outs" are really for. Baseball is a team sport, therefore, the only thing you can control is

NOTES

your mental state of mind.

Trying too hard (showstopper #2)

If one word should be eliminated from your vocabulary, it should be the word *trying.* Whenever you catch yourself about to say, "I'm trying....", change it to: "I'm **being**," "I'm" **doing"** or "I'm **allowing**." You are simply *allowing* your hero character to emerge. You are *being* the character. You are *doing* what comes naturally to your character. You are *allowing* your story to unfold. "Trying" opens up a Pandora's Box of unnecessary thinking. It puts you in a place of judging, defining and evaluating. It's nowhere near the zone.

Not minding what happens

Remember, **you've** written the story. You **know** how the story ends. Although the details are handled for you, it's the details that make your story colorful, interesting, and funny-a real page turner. Judging or defining any of the details only attracts more *like* thoughts. These thoughts usually snowball into alternate scenarios or deviations from your script. Sometimes, a

NOTES

detail, to a judgmental mind, may appear to be a disappointment. To the non-judgmental mind, it is merely one of those twists and turns that keeps you engaged and intrigued along your journey. When unexpected details arise, appreciate them and be entertained by them, but don't judge or label them as good or bad. Rather than being attached to a desired outcome, *don't mind what happens!*

As an example, imagine it's your first at bat in a big game. The first pitch comes and it's in the dirt. The Umpire yells, "strike one", clearly not the call you wanted or expected to hear! If you let yourself decide, "That's a terrible call", that thought instantly generates negative emotions. By judging the call as bad, you have taken yourself out of the zone. Even by mentally celebrating a bad call that benefits you, you exit the zone. Simply observing from a place of non-thinking and allowing your autopilot (subconscious) to take over will keep you focused and in the zone.

NOTES

Repeat this to yourself. **The zone is a place of non-thinking. It is the gap between the last thought you had (past) and the next one you will have (future).**

<u>Charlie's Story</u>

I have a friend who is a professional UFC fighter. Although he trains all year round, the months preceding a fight are extremely intense. Two days before a very important fight he was informed that his opponent was dropping out due to an injury. Instead of judging the situation as negative or getting discouraged, he simply relayed to his fans, "I apologize to my fans who bought tickets and booked hotels and airfare. But I <u>know</u> that nothing ever happens for no reason."

Charlie was still required to travel to the venue city and weigh in the day before the event, in order to get paid for the fight. Just hours before the weigh-ins, one of the fighters on the main card became unable to fight. Out of nowhere, Charlie was offered a Main Event fight against a much higher ranked opponent, on national television! Of course he seized the opportunity. He went on to win by a Unanimous Decision.

NOTES

Charlie's career took a gigantic leap that night. By keeping his focus on what he wanted and not dwelling on what seemed like a bad turn of events, he was able to recognize the new opportunity when it presented itself.

Many of his fans cancelled their trips and ate the cost of the tickets. My Dad and I decided to go, even though Charlie was no longer scheduled to fight. We decided it would be an adventure, since we had never seen a UFC fight live. By keeping our minds open and having a sense of adventure, we experienced one of the most memorable weekends of our lives. We got to see Charlie's dream come true. . . LIVE

We all have opportunities presenting themselves on a regular basis. Those "coincidences" you experience are not accidents. They are all opportunities you notice because your attention is in the right place. You are observing in the present moment. If you are complaining, worrying or fussing about "the details", the opportunities still come, you just don't see them.

NOTES

Needing the approval of others
(showstopper #3)

Last summer I had the privilege of witnessing the first flight of a baby Blue Jay. The scene began with the Momma Blue Jay taking flight from the nest and flying back and forth over the nest, time and again. Her performance was in full view of her young apprentice, who sat in the nest, quietly watching. I noticed the baby's head gently tilting from side to side observing his mother's flight. I was mesmerized. I can't really say how long this went on. This real life "bird documentary" seemed to make time stand still.

This was a silent movie, as there seemed to be no communication between Teacher and Student . Instinctively, when the Mother decided the lesson was over, she landed at the nest and gently began nudging her baby out. In the next frame, I noticed a flurry of frantic wing flapping followed by the sound of a thump on the ground below the tree! Now, on the ground, the baby continued to scurry and flap his wings frantically, while his Teacher stood silently on the sidelines. The baby never stopped rehearsing the wing

NOTES

flapping he had just observed his Mother demonstrate.

Suddenly, Momma bird swiftly jetted out of the nest, landing on the fence gate. She sensed, or saw a cat approaching the yard, long before I noticed it creeping in the direction of the baby bird. She began to distract the cat by "cawcawing" over and over. Her *mantra* kept the cat at bay, focusing its attention on her, instead. The baby continued his *exercises*, until finally, he achieved liftoff!

This Birdie Blockbuster was loaded with wonder, drama, excitement and close calls. Yet, after the baby succeeded, there were no Birdie High Fives or Wing Pumps. There was only the joy of flying!

We can compare the Conscious Mind to the sneaky cat. Your attention to your breathing in Mind Exercise #2, distracts your conscious mind to allow the Subconscious Mind to do its job. If you've ever witnessed a two or three year old trying to play Frisbee with Grandma's best dishes, you know the best way to stop him is to distract him and

NOTES

direct his attention elsewhere. It is the most harmonious way to save Grandma's dishes, and keep the toddler playing joyfully at the same time. If instead, you began yelling and screaming, the child who aims to please, will, without language, label and define it as a "bad" event.

Which type of *Actor* are you?

There are many stories of Actors who seem to have no desire to be excellent at the art of acting, but are driven by the desire to be famous. Initially, they are always seen seeking attention and posing for the paparazzi. Many have some success, only to spend the rest of their careers cursing the paparazzi and their fans for their lack of privacy.

The great Actors, live only for the joy of acting. Many, almost shun public attention, and most, only take on roles they feel will be artistically rewarding and enhance their craft. We witness their greatness on the stage or screen. Like them, great ball players play for the joy and love of the game. Whether the audience likes a particular performance or not, doesn't change their love for the game

NOTES

or the joy they experience while playing.

Making adjustments

The most effective and enjoyable way to acquire any new skill is to study someone who already excels at it. Most of the skills you learned as a child came from observing others until you were comfortable enough to begin doing it yourself. That's how you learned to walk, throw a ball, and probably ride a skateboard.

Write down some examples of your own.

These are skills I acquired without any formal instruction or a Coach:

_____

_____

_____

_____

_____

_____

_____

_____

_____

_____

_____

NOTES

Mind Exercise #3

This exercise is for any fine tuning you feel would enhance your game, or your life in general.

For example, you decide you would like to fine tune your swing to add more power. Seek out the most powerful hitter on your team, or a favorite power hitter you see on TV. Start by doing the Relaxation exercises. Move on to Mind Exercise #2. Once you are in that place of non-thinking, give your subconscious the following suggestion: "I would love to have a more powerful swing."

Next, begin studying the power hitter you have chosen. Observe the details of his swing, but watch it as a whole. Your subconscious will absorb this picture/video, and start incorporating the improvements into your existing swing.

Begin experimenting and playing around with your newly modified swing until you become comfortable with it. Allow it to happen naturally. The process should be fun. The results will be fun too!

NOTES

Always, remember that you **know** how your story ends! You decided to succeed *before* you stepped onto the field. You have planted all the seeds of success. Allow The Universe to handle the details!

Congratulations! Since you have read this far and have begun mastering the exercises, you are well on your way to living your life by design.

Always, remember you were a masterpiece when you were born. You arrived on this Earth, fully equipped to have an exciting and fulfilling life.

In nature, we never see a single bird getting all the food, and the other birds going without. We never see two flowers in the garden getting all the sunshine while the others wither in darkness. All have access to everything they need at all times.

And, so it is with you. You have access to everything you desire.
>You are good enough.
>You are worthy.
>You deserve the best life has to offer as a person and as an athlete.

NOTES

By now, you realize the only true opponent you'll ever have is you.

Now that you understand the process, be sure to make your story a good one!!!

NOTES

"Nothing in this world can take the place of persistence. Talent will not; nothing is more common than unsuccessful people with talent. Genius will not; unrewarded genius is almost a proverb. Education will not; the world is full of educated derelicts. Persistence and determination alone are omnipotent. The slogan "press on" has solved and always will solve the problems of the human race."

Calvin Coolidge

ASK ELLIOT

Life is ongoing & so is this course!

For help along your exciting
journey you have company
every step of the way.

For questions, advice or to book a
workshop for your team or school

Visit our Website at

www.GettingIntoTheZone.com

or email to:

AskElliot@GettingIntoTheZone.com

Recommended reading

The Secret | by Rhonda Byrne

The Way of the Peaceful
Warrior | by Dan Millman

The Power of Your
Subconscious Mind | by Joseph Murphy

The Magic of Thinking Big | by David J.
Schwartz, PhD

Mind Gym | by Gary Mack

Videos

The Secret | Rhonda Byrne

Peaceful Warrior | Dan Millman

What the Bleep
Do we know? | Arnst, Chase,
Vincent

About the Authors

Elliot Hagburg earned his Business Management degree at Hofstra University via Division I Baseball. He coaches and trains High School Athletes and is a certified personal trainer.

Kathy Hagburg is retired with thirty years experience in sales, management, business and personal training.

24075805R00052

Made in the USA
Lexington, KY
04 July 2013